Bringing Home the Prodigals

ROB PARSONS

Hodder & Stoughton
LONDON SYDNEY AUCKLAND

Unless otherwise indicated, Scripture quotations are taken from the HOLY BIBLE, NEW INTERNATIONAL VERSION. Copyright © 1973, 1978, 1984 by International Bible Society. Used by permission of Hodder & Stoughton. All rights reserved. "NIV" is a registered trademark of International Bible Society. UK trademark number 1448790.

Copyright © 2003 by Rob Parsons

First published in Great Britain in 2003

The right of Rob Parsons to be identified as the Author of the Work has been asserted by him in accordance with the Copyright, Designs and Patents Act 1988.

10 9 8 7 6 5 4 3

British Library Cataloguing in Publication Data
A record for this book is available from the British Library

ISBN 0 340 86115 0

Printed and bound in Great Britain by Clays Ltd, St Ives plc

The paper and board used in this paperback are natural recyclable products made from wood grown in sustainable forests. The manufacturing processes conform to the environmental regulations of the country of origin.

Hodder & Stoughton
A Division of Hodder Headline Ltd
338 Euston Road
London NW1 3BH

www.madaboutbooks.com

The *Bringing Home the Prodigals* project has received commendations from a wide variety of Christian leaders. Here are just a few:

'This book is a gift to the whole Church.'
Dr R. T. Kendall,
former Minister at Westminster Chapel, London

'*Bringing Home the Prodigals* is both deeply practical and deeply moving; it reacquaints us with the very centre of the Gospel of Jesus.'
Dr Rowan Williams,
Archbishop of Canterbury

'It is true that the task of evangelism is a vital one, but we must not take our eye off the great tragedy of those who leave the Church. I believe there is something very special about this project and I am thrilled that it has begun.'
Joel Edwards,
General Director, Evangelical Alliance

'I support this initiative with all my heart. *Bringing Home the Prodigals* has many aspects: a releasing from guilt, a challenge to the local church to be communities of love, and an examination of what really matters to God. But above all, this is a nationwide call to prayer that God in His mercy will touch the lives of our prodigals wherever they are – and bring them home.'
Rev. David Coffey,
General Secretary of the Baptist Union,
Free Church Moderator, and Co-President of Churches
Together in Britain and Ireland

'There is no greater challenge to the modern church than bringing home the prodigals. There is hardly a family in our nation that is not touched by this issue. I can't tell you how excited I am by the incredible prospect of seeing tens of thousands of our prodigals coming home.'

Rev. John Glass,
General Superintendent of the Elim Pentecostal Church

'As a father and a father-in-God,
I welcome Rob Parsons' *Bringing Home the Prodigals* initiative. It must be seen, however, not only as changing the direction of those who have left their spiritual 'homes', but also as a major challenge to churches to become truly places of grace, welcome and forgiveness. When both these changes take place together, the possibilities, under God, are enormous!'

The Rt Rev. Harold Miller,
Bishop of Down and Dromore

'Spring Harvest are thrilled to be a part of this God-inspired initiative. We pray that many prodigals will return to their First Love.'

Alan Johnson,
Chief Executive, Spring Harvest

'Church should be the place where everyone feels safe, loved and accepted. So often this is not the case. To quote Rob, "We have all made it easier for our prodigals to leave … and, saddest of all, made it harder for them to return." I believe that we

need to reflect the love of our heavenly Father and address the challenges outlined in this book. We must make it easier for people to recognise the boundless, unconditional love of God. I pray that we may witness thousands returning home.'
Lieutenant-Colonel Robert Halliday,
Territorial Evangelism Secretary, The Salvation Army

'We believe that God, in His mercy, is powerfully using *Bringing Home the Prodigals* to touch tens of thousands of hearts and homes and churches everywhere.'
Lyndon and Celia Bowring
– Lyndon is the Executive Chairman of CARE,
Celia is an international speaker

'There are thousands of disillusioned and hurting people who need to return home to our churches. *Bringing Home the Prodigals* points us towards a loving community of believers humbly praying for their return. It is my prayer that thousands return to accepting churches who take responsibility to help them on their onward journey.'
Rev. Stuart Bell,
Ground Level Team Leader

'This book helpfully goes to the heart of what makes relationships work and offers hope for anyone feeling that there is no way back to God.'
Peter Kerridge,
Managing Director, Premier Christian Radio

Contents

Dedication   *ix*

Acknowledgements   *x*

Always Leave a Light on   *1*

CHAPTER ONE
Who Are the Prodigals?   *7*

CHAPTER TWO
Before They Are Prodigals   *21*

CHAPTER THREE
Let Go of False Guilt   *37*

CHAPTER FOUR
It's Time to Stop Judging and Start Sharing   *59*

CHAPTER FIVE
Release the Life-Changing Power of Forgiveness   *69*

CHAPTER SIX
Get the Home Ready for Their Return   *79*

CHAPTER SEVEN
The Patience to Wait and the Grace to Accept   *95*

CHAPTER EIGHT
Praying Home the Prodigals   *109*

Dedication

To Sheron Rice, who has worked alongside me for over twelve years, with more thanks than I can possibly say. You are one of God's gifts to me.

And to my friend Rhys Williams. May you fulfil your dreams. Keep the faith.

Acknowledgements

Many people have helped with *Bringing Home the Prodigals* but special thanks to Jonathan Booth, Sheron Rice, Steve Williams, Andrew Cooper, Kate Hancock and the people at Prayer for Revival who began it all. The team at Hodder & Stoughton have been brilliant; special thanks to Judith Longman, Charles Nettleton, Julie Hatherall and Patrick Knowles.

Thank you also to those who contributed prayers and reflections, especially Wendy Bray who bore the lion's share of that.

We gratefully acknowledge permission to use the following poems:

The poem on p. 36 is taken from *When Life Takes What Matters* by Susan Lenzkes, copyright © 1993. Used by permission of Discovery House Publishers, Box 3566, Grand Rapids, Michigan 49501. All rights reserved.

The poem on p. 50 is taken from *Prodigals and Those Who Love Them* by Ruth Bell Graham, copyright © 1991. Used by permission of Focus on Family Publishing, Colorado Springs, CO 80935 3550. All rights reserved.

And finally, thank you to those who allowed their stories to be told.

Always Leave a Light on

I wrote part of this book in a small conference centre on the Gower coast near Swansea. The building is set on a hill and the view from my window was unspeakably beautiful, running across fields, then woods and finally ending at the sea in the great sweep of Oxwich Bay. One morning I took a break from writing and stood outside the house gazing into the distance at the breakers hitting the beach. After a few minutes I was joined by a priest. He had on the traditional long black cassock, had a flowing grey beard, and wore what my kids used to call 'Jesus sandals'. He had been leading a discussion in one of the seminar rooms and said he had 'just come out to get a little air while they ponder a couple of theological teasers I've set them'.

He told me a most moving story

We began chatting and he asked me what I was doing. When I told him I was writing a book about prodigals he told me a most moving story. Let me try to capture his words as I remember them:

None of us have ever seen that house without a light on

> *In a village near here, is a large old house. An elderly lady lives there alone and every night, as darkness falls, she puts a light on in the attic. Her son left home twenty-five years ago, rather like the prodigal in the parable, but she has never given up the hope that one day he will come home. We all know the house well, and although the bulb must occasionally need replacing, none of us have ever seen that house without a light on. It is for her son.*

All over the world I have cried with parents for their prodigals. There is no more fervent prayer in homes today than, 'Father, bring home our prodigal.' I have concentrated in this book on those who have children – of whatever age – who are prodigals, but of course there are many kinds of prodigal – brothers, sisters, husbands, wives and friends. I hope with all my heart that whoever is on your heart you will find something here to encourage you and keep the flames of hope alight.

This book is certainly not written principally as a book of advice, although I will share with you the lessons I have learned from many whose hearts are crying out to God for those they love. My hope is that it will be a book that will release us from false guilt, bring us hope and above all lead us to prayer. At the end of every chapter is a prayer and reflection; each one is written by somebody who has cried for a prodigal and who has come to believe that ultimately God is our only hope. At the very end of the book we will each bring our prodigals to the cross of Christ.

But I confess that it was not just parents, family or friends of prodigals that I had in mind as I wrote this book, for I believe that many of us in the Christian community have some heart-searching to do in this area. We have all, at times, made it easier for our prodigals to leave, kept them out of mind when they are gone and, saddest of all, made it harder

We have all, at times, made it easier for our prodigals to leave

for them to come home. At our very worst we have been the elder brother. But we can change. We can catch the Father's heart for the prodigals; the outrageous grace of the one who, even as we stumble down the long road home, runs to throw a robe on our back, put a ring on our finger and shoes on our feet. And if we do change, if we can catch something of that father-heart of God, then it may be that, in his great mercy, he will touch the lives of thousands of our prodigals – and bring them home.

Love from the Father

When the night fell
When the stars shone
When the thin clouds dusted
When the air was cold
When the world was quiet
I sat on the grass and thought
About who I was and what I did.
And I was scared.
I thought about how I was wrong
How carelessly I hurt people
How I was cruel to those I love.
I looked at the stars searchingly
And I found myself asking God to forgive me.
I sat in silence listening to everything
But hearing nothing.
Then God touched me, lifted me.
I walked home and found a note,
A message on my door.
I forgive you my child, love from the father.

A seventeen-year-old boy
(it was his first poem)

CHAPTER ONE

Who Are the Prodigals?

It is true that the parable of the prodigal son is two thousand years old, but it is being re-enacted every day in homes all across our world as thousands of mothers and fathers wait up until the early hours of the morning for their children to come home. It is being relived in the homes where in the children's bedrooms the drugs were first found, being played out again in the tears, the pain and the sheer frustration of the broken dreams and the crying out of, 'Where did we go wrong?'

This simple parable has been called the greatest short story in the world

This is a modern story. Perhaps it is *our* story for, of a certainty, there is no family, no matter how godly, how expert at parenting, or how devoted to each other, which is immune from the circumstances that cause us to cry out to God for our children.

This simple parable has been called the greatest short story in the world. It is the tale of the boy who broke his father's heart and yet could not destroy the love the father had for him. We find it difficult in our modern culture to take in the full impact of what this young man did. He was not just seeking to sow a few wild oats; he was turning his back on everything his father, his community, and his very upbringing, had taught him. He would not, in the time-honoured way of Eastern communities, wait for his father to die before he received

The money runs out, the friends leave, and he is destitute

his inheritance. He wanted it all now. In essence he was saying, 'I wish you were dead already.'

And the boy gets his money and goes to what Dr Luke calls 'a distant country' – as far as he can possibly get from his father, from the influences and the things that restricted him at home. In fact he goes so far from his Jewish roots that in this place they keep pigs. He has more money than he ever dreamt of and more friends than he ever hoped for, and whatever we want to make of it, this boy is having fun. He's partying as if it's going out of fashion and you get the feeling that he wished he'd left the old man's house earlier. And then it happens:

Apart from death, there was nowhere else for this young man to go

the money runs out, the friends leave, and he is destitute – not just economically, but socially and spiritually. He is in the pits – and he's alone.

It would have been hard for Jesus to have painted a more graphic illustration for a Jewish audience of how low this boy had sunk than for him to have told them that the boy found himself in a pigsty, debating whether or not to eat the animals' food. Those who listened that day understood the message well: apart from death, there was nowhere else for this young man to go.

But as the boy sat in that sty something happened. If the money had not run out, or if the famine had not come, it might not have occurred, but one day 'he came to his senses'. And the second he did, his mind went back to home. It was the tragedy of his situation that eventually cleared his mind, it was the hunger that made him consider going home, and it was the shame that made him decide on the speech. He would go to his father and say, 'I have sinned against heaven and against you.' As he put the words together some of those sins came flooding back to him and he added, 'I am no longer worthy to be called your son. Make me like one of the hired servants.' He reasoned that if he came back as a servant then at least his father could kick him out if he wanted to – the hired help could be dismissed at a day's notice, they had even less status than the slaves. And so he began the long walk home.

And that is how it would have ended – with a boy coming back full of shame, eating humble pie, and a father saying, 'I told you so – why didn't you listen to your mother and me?' It *would* have ended just like that except for one thing: the father had never given up on him. He had never stopped looking down the road and he had never stopped loving.

The father had never given up on him

And because the father had never given up hope, then before the boy saw him, he saw the boy. And he began to run. As he reached him, he threw his arms around him and began kissing him. The young man tried to begin his speech but never did manage to finish it – never did get to the part that said, 'I am no longer worthy to be called your son' – because the old man was shouting to the servants: 'Quick! Put a robe on his back, a ring on his finger and shoes on his feet! Start preparing a party! My boy's home!'

The making of a prodigal

It is without doubt a wonderful story and the important question for us is, 'Who are the prodigals today?' The truth is that we have made 'prodigals' of some who never were in the first place.

It is a great tragedy that in the modern church so often we judge each other by rules and regulations that we have devised ourselves and which have

We have made 'prodigals' of some who never were in the first place

nothing to do with following Christ. And so often it is with this unwritten code that we 'create' our prodigals. In various Christian cultures across the world a person can be written off as a prodigal over something that in another culture is accepted. I remember an older man telling us that when he was a boy he used to help his father give out tracts entitled, 'Should Baptists dance?' There is many a church leader who has been approached by a representative of the deaconate or the PCC saying, 'Pastor, we say this in love, but some of us are very worried about the behaviour of your children. We've noticed that one of them has body-piercing/ dresses all in black/started smoking/goes to nightclubs.'

And so it begins – the making of a prodigal.

In the eyes of the religious leaders of his time, Jesus himself was a prodigal There is nothing new in this. In every age there have been those who are more concerned with religion than faith and who are quick to point out where somebody has missed *their* particular mark. The Pharisees came to Jesus and said, 'Why do your disciples eat with unwashed hands?' and 'Why don't your disciples fast?' They were saying, 'Your own people are going off the road – what are you going to do about it?'

In the eyes of the religious leaders of his time, Jesus himself was a prodigal. They noted that he ate with sinners. Time and time again they reminded him of their own adherence to the rules and regulations that, in their eyes, meant they were right with God, but this didn't stop Jesus living his life outside of the protection of the religious ghetto. It's easy for some Christians to see others as prodigals because they themselves live in such an unreal world. Some of our young people who are written off as prodigals are at least trying to follow Christ in a world that exists outside of the Christian goldfish bowl. In contrast, many Christians not only don't have one friend that doesn't share their Christian faith – they don't have one friend that doesn't share their *particular brand* of the Christian faith.

And who are the prodigals anyway?

And who are the prodigals anyway? Consider this: a man has two sons. Both seem to be followers of Christ although the younger one, Jack, has always been something of a rebel. It was Jack who slipped a goldfish into the baptistry and, yes, it was he who, when he was twelve, put vodka into the speaker's water jar on the pulpit. Stephen, on the other hand, seemed a model child and in later life – and true to form – he never did rock the boat very much.

When he was twenty years old Jack stopped going to church. He found it so hard to fit in and often felt more of a sense of fellowship in the pub than he ever did in the prayer-meeting. Eventually he left home and moved to a big city.

He immediately started to work with homeless people. It was hard work. He was often conned out of the little money he earned, was beaten up twice, and was once arrested for standing up for a woman who slept in a shop doorway and was about to have her few possessions put onto a skip outside an Oxford Street store. Jack had a wonderful heart for people. Sometimes their pain would make him cry.

The other son, Stephen, never stopped going to church. In fact Stephen rarely missed any meeting at all and it wasn't long before he was asked to join the deaconate. Here he proved to be efficient and dedicated – and a complete pain. He spoke to people badly, was ungracious, and made the church leader's life an absolute misery. Stephen had strong opinions on how things should be done and often said, 'It's important to have high standards for the sake of the church.' People frequently found it hard to meet those standards – whether it was the worship leader, the youth pastor or the single-parent mum whose kids would sometimes disturb the family service – and when they failed, Stephen told them so.

Which of those two sons was a prodigal? The answer is both. And both needed to come home.

Which of those two sons was a prodigal? The answer is both

But before we go any further it is absolutely vital that we define what 'coming home' means. I believe that church attendance is important – almost every Sunday of my life I am in my own church – but church attendance is not the only way to try to decide whether somebody is a prodigal or not. In Christian circles if somebody asks us how our kids are doing spiritually, then so long as they attend church on Sunday and one mid-week meeting that seems to give us the right to say, 'I'm pleased to say they are following Christ.' But do they care for the poor? Do they *love* Christ? Do they stand up for injustice when they see it? Can they forgive or do they harbour grudges? Are they compassionate? Patient? And is there any evidence that slowly they are becoming a little more like the one they follow?

We desperately need God's wisdom in dealing with this. We dare not get it wrong for, if we do, we not only allow some in deep spiritual need to remain in their complacency but we also drive away those who never did turn their back on God at all. I fear that there is many a child who hears regularly from her parents that they are praying for her to return to God, but who really needs to hear their encouragement for the things she is doing that please God.

We drive away those who never did turn their back on God at all

The great problem with the church in the Western world is that half the prodigals are still in the pews. It's true that our wrongs may not be as easy to see as those of others, but in our hearts we know that we are as far away: the boy in the parable wasted his life in riotous living – we are eaten away with bitterness; he wasted his money – we hoard it; he gave his body to prostitutes – we sacrifice our mind to pornography.

What ultimately saved the boy in the parable is that he came to despair of his life and craved what he had known at home. Many of us have never known that despair – but we should have. Somebody put it like this, 'Our churches are filled with nice, kind, loving people, who have never known the despair of guilt or the breathless wonder of forgiveness.'

Before we pray for them to come home, let's make sure they are really gone

The only way the religious establishment could accuse Jesus of being a prodigal was because they had no idea of what really mattered to God. And it was for this reason they found it so hard to contemplate the awful possibility that in reality it was he who was in the Father's house and they who were left outside.

Before we pray for them to come home, let's make sure they are really gone.

Prayer

Lord, unclench my fist, my hand,
Prise open my fingers,
Break the habit of a lifetime
Years of comforting, providing.

Lord, release my thoughts,
Prise open my mind,
Let me trust you with this precious child.

Lord, have I trapped him by my love?
Too close, too tight.
Have I edged you out, forgetting
You knew him before he was born?
You loved him before I did?

He's yours, Lord,
I release him to you.

Reflection

Stop your crying and wipe away your tears.
All that you have done for your children will not go unrewarded;
they will return from the enemy's land.
There is hope for your future;
your children will come back home.
I, the Lord, have spoken.

Jeremiah 31:16–17 *(Good News)*

God identifies with our tears at the absence of our prodigals. He shares them. But he promises us that all of our efforts and longings as parents, grandparents, husbands, wives, brothers, sisters or friends do not go unnoticed by him. He assures us that he is in control and that he can be trusted with their lives, wherever they wander. There is hope.

CHAPTER TWO

Before They Are Prodigals

A mother and father approached me during an event at which I was speaking in North America. They were in their early sixties and their daughter was seventeen. The father said to me, 'We're so worried about our daughter. She's always pushed the boundaries, but now she likes to go dancing on a Friday night.'

'Well,' I thought to myself, 'at least she sounds normal.'

The father went on, 'Sometimes she likes to go dancing on a Saturday night as well.'

'We're so worried about our daughter'

'You know,' I said, 'that's pretty ordinary behaviour for a teenager. There are lots of dangers out there but I've no doubt you've instilled in your daughter what's right and wrong, and in just a few months she'll be an adult.'

The mother said, 'But she refuses to go to the youth Bible study.'

As they spoke I could imagine the scene in their house – this teenager coming downstairs and her parents saying, 'You can't go out looking like that,' or the rows over whether she can go out again on the Saturday having already been out on the Friday night. My heart went out to this older couple who were doing all they could to keep their girl on the right path, but with the effort practically killing them.

'What's your daughter like around the house?' I asked.

'She's fine,' the mother replied. 'But as I said, she won't go to the youth Bible study.'

Praise her for what she is doing right

'Does she ever go to church with you?' I asked, expecting them to say no, not since she was twelve. They replied, 'Every Sunday – she never misses.'

'Do you mean to tell me that every Sunday, regardless of how late she comes home the night before, she is in church the next day?' I asked.

'Yes,' they answered. 'Every Sunday.'

'That's incredible!' I said. 'When you go home tonight I want you to say to your daughter, "Darling, we were telling somebody about you tonight and the fact that you are so very faithful every Sunday in coming to church. We felt proud of you."'

I will never forget what happened next. The mother looked at me and said, 'Mr Parsons, didn't you hear what we said a moment ago? She won't go to the youth Bible study!'

'Forget that for the moment' I said. 'Don't always be criticising her for what you think she is doing wrong. Praise her for what she is doing right – because if you don't, you're going to have more to worry about than the youth Bible study. It seems to me that at the moment this child is trying to honour God as best she can and she needs every encouragement in that. Don't make a prodigal of your daughter over some mid-week meeting.'

'Don't make a prodigal of your daughter over some mid-week meeting'

Most families have a child who, in their younger years, looks more likely to become a prodigal. I sometimes wonder if it becomes a self-fulfilling prophecy in that we set them such impossible standards. We require them to jump through hoops they were never designed to negotiate and eventually they give up trying. They think to themselves, 'If my parents really think I'm so bad then I may as well prove them right.'

If you have more than one child they will almost certainly be completely different to each other. That is particularly hard if your first child was compliant because, for a while, you thought you were the perfect parents. The first loved helping with the washing up, spent hours tidying her room, and saved up her pocket money to buy study guides. The second is a little different. This little boy wakes up every morning and says to himself, 'How can I drive my mother crazy today?' He goes to bed worried that he hasn't made a good job of it.

How can I drive my mother crazy today?

In most homes you will find that the majority of the discipline, the sanctions, the curfews and the rows are centred on that more testing child. These actions may well be necessary but there are dangers. I remember my son Lloyd saying to me when he was about sixteen years old, 'Dad, I know it's not true now, but when I was young I used to think you loved Katie more than me.'

'I understand that, son,' I said, 'because whenever pandemonium broke out you were in the middle of it, and in addition I now realise that your big sister used to sneak some of her mischief onto you!'

Find something in which we can encourage them – find something they can do well

We simply have to break the cycle where the only words such a child hears from us are negative. It is imperative to find something in which we can encourage them – perhaps let them overhear us praising them to others. It will help if we find something they can do well that their 'Goody Two-Shoes' sibling can't. It may be a hobby or a sport – anything that gives them dignity in their own right. Work hard to find this skill in them – it is absolutely vital. The alternative is for them to choose rebellion as the way of gaining a little significance. And, above all, we need to let them know in a hundred ways that although at times it seems to be constant warfare between us, we couldn't love them more.

I remember having lunch with a company director and asking him to tell me about his family.

'I've got three kids' he replied. 'My eldest daughter is twenty-five and she's doing a PhD; the second girl is twenty-two and she's doing an MA.' With that he picked up his knife and starting eating. I said, 'Tell me about your third child.'

'Oh,' he replied. 'My son's nineteen. He's dyslexic. He doesn't work hard at college, his bedroom's a mess, he gets parking tickets and forgets to pay them. I tell him he'd better sharpen up – it's a tough world out there.'

I asked, 'Can you remember when you last praised that boy for anything at all?'

He replied, 'No, I really can't.'

I said, 'When you go home, find something that boy has done remotely well and praise him for it. It will revolutionise your relationship with him.' To his credit he said that he would.

I think of another man who approached me at the end of a business seminar. He told me that he had a very poor relationship with his nineteen-year-old daughter. I asked him what gifts his daughter had, and he replied that she was a fantastic singer. I asked him if he had ever told her he was proud of the way she sings. He replied, 'Never'. I urged him to do it that very day.

We all need to be praised more than we dare acknowledge

We all need to be praised more than we dare acknowledge and, for our children, it is absolutely vital. It's good to know that even if your parents are on your back most of the time, you can, occasionally, make them proud.

The great danger for any parent is that the desire to let a child know how strongly we disapprove will be greater than the impulse that lets them know that no matter what they have done, they are still loved. I have heard parents in church making negative comments about their children's dress, facial ironmongery or colour of hair – and in front of those children. Maybe they are trying to say, 'I know he looks like this/goes there/smokes but I don't approve.' Did we honestly think our friends thought all along that we were filled with enthusiasm for that pin through our daughter's lower lip? The price we pay for that little piece of self-justification is that our children come to believe that although we tell them we love them – that actually we don't *accept* them.

Unconditional love is one of the most powerful forces on the face of the earth

I am always thrilled when I am in a church and notice a wild-looking teenager in the worship band. As I watch him or her play I have no doubt in my mind that they'd rather be backing the Stereophonics but, nevertheless, this church has embraced them as they are – the way they look, the gifts they have – and said, 'Be part of us. Bring your worship to God in your way.'

Unconditional love is one of the most powerful forces on the face of the earth. But it can be very hard to give. One parent wrote:

> *I know there is no greater force than love, but we have loved our son until it has broken us. We have bailed him out of police cells and had drug*

dealers call at our home and threaten us. He has stolen from us, abused us, and brought us close to the edge of insanity. Sometimes we feel so guilty because we feel it would have been better if he had died. At least then he would be safe. But still we love. We cannot help loving. Only God can help us to love like that.

'We have loved our son until it has broken us'

There are some things we can do to help that more challenging child, but there's quite a lot we cannot do. And therefore, if we are wise, we will allow other adults – friends of ours, youth leaders, sports leaders – to play a part in moulding our children's lives. It's hard because especially during their teen years our children may go through periods when they confide more readily in these 'significant others' than in us. What can be even more galling is that they are happy to be seen walking down the street with these people – even though they may be as old and boring-looking as we are – but they wouldn't be seen out dead with us. The truth is that it's easier for these people – they don't have to deal with the 24-hour-a-day pressure and hassles, or grapple with any discipline issues. Nevertheless their role is crucial. The breakdown in the extended family, and the increasing isolation in which many families live, has made such people harder to find – but find them we must.

Parenting is a long-haul business and our children may yet surprise us

But in the midst of it all, and whether right now our kids are easy to live with or whether they are driving us crazy, we would do well to remember that parenting is a long-haul business and our children may yet surprise us. And for that very reason we shouldn't read the score at half-time. That testing child can change and the really big shock is that the compliant one normally has a surprise or two up her sleeve as well – just enough to say, 'Don't take me for granted. I can keep you awake at night as well.'

And don't despair of sowing good seed into their lives. Even that more challenging child is taking in more than you think. One of the most encouraging and sobering aspects of parenting is not only how much our children remember of what we taught them, but that they actually eventually put it into practice in their own lives *as though they had thought of it themselves.*

If you doubt what I say then think how often you find yourself repeating advice that your parents once gave you which, somewhere between your teens years and however old you are now, moved from your disbelieving it, through to your ignoring it, to finally not only adopting it as your own but actively promoting it as the best way to do things.

Sowing seeds in our children's lives when they are small – Bible passages, stories of heroes and heroines of the faith, singing songs with them that can inspire them to faith in God – go deep into the soil of their very being. There is many a prodigal who at their lowest moment remembered a line from an old hymn or a verse from the Bible that caused them to find hope again and a way back. Don't be discouraged. Many a seed that seemed destined to die has somehow fought against rock and frost to find a way to life. My mother had green fingers. She could take a plant that others would

Even that more challenging child is taking in more than you think

have thrown on the rubbish heap and coax it back to life. Don't give up on that seed.

Remember the words of Jesus: 'My Father is the gardener.'

Prayer

Father God
Look at my son.
He is unique – and how! There is no
one else like him.
I cannot fathom him – or his ways.
But you know all of them.
You know his heart, his dreams.
If I have judged him by my standards
instead of yours, forgive me.
If I have expected too much, been swift to
criticise and slow to listen, I'm sorry.
Help me understand his way with you,
and yours with him.
Help me accept that he does not need a
pew to sit at your feet
May not always need to do the done
thing – just your thing,
That the songs he sings can be sung
in a different tune.
I cannot watch his every move, plant
his every step.
But your hand is on him wherever he goes
Until he really 'comes home'.

Reflection

Man looks at the outward appearance, but the Lord looks at the heart.

1 Samuel 16:7b

God often uses the most unconventional of his children in ways we could never have expected. His focus is the heart and motivation of those who claim to love and follow him, not their qualifications, charisma or congeniality. Our ability to accept that God may act in surprising ways through surprising people – especially the young – is a measure of our spiritual maturity.

Pain is a language,
without words —
and so it is untouched
by words.

Does it help to know
that my prayers for you
are often wordless too?

And shaped like tears.

Susan Lenzkes

We do not know what we ought to pray for, but
the Spirit himself intercedes for us with groans
that words cannot express ...

Romans 8:26

CHAPTER THREE

Let Go of False Guilt

There is no pain like parental pain. The love of a parent for a child is like no other. Our children can disappoint us, hurt us, even abuse us, but somehow we cannot stop loving them. Sometimes it seems that the more they cause us to worry the more we love them. We would willingly give our lives for these children.

And yet sometimes that love can be very hard to give. I well remember a woman telling me that her thirteen-year-old daughter had driven her to despair. She said, 'I hear other parents talk with sadness about the day when their kids leave home and the nest will be empty and yet I cannot wait for my daughter to go. I can't honestly tell you that I do *feel* love for this

> *The love of a parent for a child is like no other*

child.' But something was driving this woman to tell her story to a stranger and I am convinced it was a cry for help that said, 'Help me to love this girl, who at times I feel has ruined my life. She has broken my heart yet she is part of me – I cannot live without loving her.'

We cannot live their lives for them

And yet as much as we love them, as much as we want their good, as much as we would give all that we possess for their sakes, we cannot live their lives for them. Our children make choices. And sometimes those choices are bad ones.

A couple come to my mind. They are church leaders and wonderful parents. Some years ago they sat with their sixteen-year-old daughter in a prison cell. She had just been arrested for burglary. I will never forget the simplicity of what they said to her in the cell that night: 'Annie, you are breaking our hearts, but you will never stop us loving you.'

I am sure that those parents would willingly have changed places with their child in that cell. But even if it had been possible, it might not have been for the best. We are their parents; we have spent all our lives making things right for them, but at times even we have to step back a little and let them learn the lessons of life. Sometimes the pain is part of the coming home.

But that doesn't stop us feeling that somehow we are responsible. The parable of the prodigal son is the third story of a trilogy. In the first there is a lost sheep, and in the second a lost coin. It would be hard to blame the sheep (and certainly the coin!) for getting lost but this story is different. Here the boy is capable of making a decision and does so – to turn his back on the father and the father's house. He, himself, *chooses*. And yet in spite of the fact that our children make their own choices, we so often feel the guilt ourselves.

'Where did we go wrong?'

I have heard that guilt voiced by parents all across the world. One couple will say, 'Where did we go wrong? Would it be different if we'd been firmer with them?' Another will say, 'Perhaps we were too rigid.' A woman will say, 'If only we'd had daily devotions with our children,' and another will whisper, 'Perhaps we forced our faith on them too much.' The guilt is gut-wrenching, all-pervasive, and sometimes causes us to simply freeze in fear for our children.

We look at other families who seem to be doing so well. We meet people who say, 'All four of my children are keen Christians' and we think, 'It must be me. How come I got it so wrong?' And at times it seems so unfair. We see homes where the parents appear to have hardly bothered at all and yet their kids seem to be a cross between Mother Teresa and Hudson Taylor.

They both sank to the floor and cried until it got dark

And sometimes the Christian community doesn't help a lot.

When David and Carla walked into church on that Sunday in June they didn't exactly feel like worshipping but at least they were there. It had been a tough six months. Just after lunch on New Year's Eve their seventeen-year-old had declared that she was leaving home to live with a thirty-year-old man whom she had met at a Christmas party the week before. They had begged her not to go. In fact David had physically held her back in the hall of their home as she struggled, suitcase in hand, to get through the door. Louise had sworn, bitten and kicked until one of their neighbours had banged on the door to see what was happening. Finally David and Carla had no choice. As they watched her get into the car they both sank to the floor and cried until it got dark.

Two months later their son, aged nineteen, called from university to say he was quitting his course. He and his girlfriend had decided to hitch-hike around Europe for a while.

The preacher that Sunday was a visitor. He began by telling the congregation about his family. He had been married for twenty-seven years and had four children aged between eighteen and twenty-five. All were, as he put it, 'Walking with the Lord' and doing well in their studies – two of them already training for missionary service overseas. Carla didn't hear a word of the sermon. She was too busy thinking, 'When did it start to unravel?' 'Where did we go wrong?' and 'How can I get out of this church without talking to anybody?'

'How can I get out of this church without talking to anybody?'

There are thousands of parents who feel like this. Parents of teenagers, parents of twenty-somethings, and elderly parents whose middle-aged children are still managing to break their hearts. And sometimes the hurt can come out of a clear blue sky. Like the father who told me this:

My wife and I had just come out of church on a Sunday morning when my mobile went. It was my best friend ringing from a police station to tell me my son had just been arrested. I felt my knees give way. As my friend handed his phone to my son and I waited for him to come on the line I remember thinking, 'I've got just one chance to get this right.'

'With God's help we will come through this'

I could hear my son crying on the other end of the phone. My first reaction was to yell at him, but the words I actually spoke seemed to belong to somebody else. 'Son, I am ashamed of what you have done but I am not ashamed of you. I love you. With God's help we will come through this.'

And as if parenting wasn't hard enough anyway, modern society practically forces us to see our children's lives as a judgment on whether or not *we* have been successful. We want our children to do well because we want to be well-thought-of ourselves. So often, when our children go through tough times – whether it's unexpectedly poor examination results or some much more serious issue – our first thought is, 'What will people think of us?'

'The greatest need is my son's wellbeing, not my reputation'

One church leader, realising that this was happening to him, put it like this: 'My boy is going through a hard time right now and my main concern was, "What will my congregation think?" But I only have just enough emotional energy to deal with the real issues and I've decided that I have to set myself free of what others think. The greatest need is my son's wellbeing, not my reputation.'

Only more honesty among us will set us free from the tyranny of the fear of what others will think; only less judging, more praying and the realisation that God, the *perfect* parent, is a *hurting* parent. And all of us would do well not to crow too loud when our kids are doing well. Marie Anne Blakely put it well, 'A mother is neither proud nor arrogant because she knows that any moment the headmaster may ring to say that her son has just ridden a motor-cycle through the school gymnasium.'

'I've been a failure as a father'

Some years ago Dr R.T. Kendall, then the senior minister at Westminster Chapel in London, was asked by the Billy Graham organisation if they could film him for an hour talking about theology. Dr Kendall talked to camera about some of the issues he used to tackle in his Friday evening 'School of Theology' classes. When they got to the end the producer said, 'We've got a couple of minutes of film left. Would you talk to us about your family?' Dr Kendall, who could be blunt to a fault, replied, 'You don't want to know about my family. I've been a failure as a father.'

I believe that R.T., as we call him, is a wonderful father, but it was his view that when his children were young he devoted too much time to his studies and to Westminster Chapel. At the time the film was made you could say that his children were prodigals. However the producer begged him to continue and so R.T. talked about those years and the mistakes he felt he had made.

The only part of the film the producers ever used – and they showed it to thousands of church leaders all across the world – was the last few minutes. It was utterly compelling. It said to others going through heartbreaking times – this is not just you.

It's no surprise they used the film in that way. I well remember hearing Dr Billy Graham talk of the years when his son Franklin was a prodigal. He said, 'Ruth and I lived in a house on top of a hill and some nights we would lie awake in the early hours of the morning waiting for Franklin to come home. Finally we would hear the car screeching its way around the bends as it came up the mountain and we would know that at least for one more night he was safe.'

So many parents are carrying a heavy load of guilt they have no right to bear

So many parents are carrying a heavy load of guilt they have no right to bear. That's not to say they have been perfect parents. They have just been *parents* – parents who have given this task their very best efforts. There's hardly a mother or father on the face of the earth who wouldn't love to have another shot at parenting – to rewind the clock and get the chance to read all the books and go to all the seminars before their children hit the teenage years – but even if we had that chance, the truth is we'd probably just make different mistakes.

And what if we could have been the *perfect* parents? The creation story brings a fascinating dimension to this. Adam and Eve had the perfect father and lived in the perfect environment but they chose a way their father didn't want them to go. In fact much of the Bible shows God, the perfect parent, saying to his children, 'Why are you turning your back on all that I have taught you?' There are no guarantees with our children. I know there is that verse in Proverbs, 'Bring up a child in the way he should go and when he is old he will not depart from it,' but that's not a guarantee, it's a general principle. If you follow it, you will give your children a wonderful foundation in life but they will still make choices.

What if we could have been the perfect parents?

It's time to lay that guilt down. You have carried it long enough. By all means ask forgiveness for those things you know you've done wrong as a parent, but then join the rest of us who have loved and guided our children as much as we could, but who, in the end, have to watch as they make their own decisions.

Ask God the father to reach out to your prodigals as only he can

There is nothing so soul-destroying as false guilt. Let it go. And begin to ask God the Father to reach out to your prodigals as only he can. Ultimately they are in his hands, not ours.

And, in truth, it was always so.

Prayer

Lord,
I have only ever loved her.
You know how that feels. To give a child
   everything and watch them throw it all
   away.
Sometimes the guilt causes me to cry
   myself to sleep,
and when I wake it is in my stomach.
I rewind the past and ask, 'What could
   we have done?'
Or sometimes, 'What if I hadn't ...?'
I watch others who are proud, sometimes,
   it seems, even boastful of their children,
Although I would not rob them of a
   moment of their pleasure.
Cut me free from what others might think
   or say. From the pain of hearing them
   congratulate themselves for the way
   their children have 'turned out'.
As if the mould she has fallen from
   was a 'second'.
Help me find a place with those who
   understand and have known this pain.

I need you to whisper to me that I did my
   best,
I was not perfect but I gave what I could.

*And, Lord, even where I failed, you
   can mend.
If I wounded, you can heal.*

*Heal me, Lord.
Lift this guilt.
Now.*

Reflection

They felt good eyes upon them
and shrank within – undone;
good parents had good children
and they – a wandering one.

The good folk never meant
to act smug or condemn,
but having prodigals
just 'wasn't done' with them.

Remind them gently, Lord,
how you
have trouble with Your children,
too.

Ruth Bell Graham

The time comes when we can no longer stagger forward with the burden guilt places on us. It is then that we must remember that God, the perfect Father, has wayward children.

Our children are ultimately God's responsibility. He is their Father. He does not ask the impossible of us. Only that we love them.

As you pray now, turn and kneel at the foot of the cross, lay down the guilt, and the crippling fear. Let God hold you.

Chris's Story

I'm now in my mid-twenties. At age five I sat on the dropped lid of a toilet and prayed with my Dad crouching beside me. It was the only quiet place we could find to ask God to come into the life of a curious, average boy with Christian parents. I remember few details except the size of the room and the fact my feet hardly touched the wooden floors. But I remember knowing that this was a big deal, I knew God was real.

A few years later I dropped and surfaced in a baptism pool, watching bubbles chase above me, trying to remember every moment in perfect detail for later reference. When I spoke in front of the assembled church I declared Jesus publicly as God – as my God. I did what thousands of Christians have been persecuted for in the safest place I could, and it was real. I didn't lie to the minister, my family or the little old ladies in the front row. And most of all I didn't lie to God. I didn't worry about tomorrow; as promised, tomorrow brought enough trouble of its own.

After that point life got thick and fast, fun and tempting, it became difficult to focus on a life which promised its rewards elsewhere. Where the church prescribed a code of conduct and an argument in support, it seemed the world had laid out life in all its fullness with all the trimmings. I was a normal teenager, I was more than a little torn.

The author Hanif Kureishi, recounting his own experience, concluded that, 'Being a child at all involves resolving, or synthesising, at least two different worlds, outlooks and positions . . . one way of coping would be to reject one world entirely, perhaps by forgetting it. Another is to be at war with it internally, trying to evacuate it, but never succeeding.' I fought that war for many years, unwilling to reject either of those two worlds. One, because it was too beautiful and tragic, it offered too much; the other, because deep down I knew it was real. God had been here, walked this earth and wanted more from me – I believed that much. However, I felt no nearer to him in the corporate gatherings of his followers than I did walking the streets at night. I didn't see God in church or nature or anywhere at all.

I hung in there, still around church, still part of the youth group if only in body but not spirit. Sermons washed over me like adverts, I saw no examples of Christians I aspired to be like, and the Bible was to me a confusing anthology of badly written morality tales. But at the hub of all this rejection, and even below a thin surface of resentment, was an unimpressive but solid sense that this was all true.

Even he slipped by unnoticed. The Jesus that I would later find so compelling managed to avoid my attention throughout every sermon my childhood notched up. I missed that fathomless, unpredictable man. I failed to notice the king who touched the poor and said he'd come to serve them, the revolutionary who turned down a plausible rebellion and opted for one which meant going silently to his grave. The perfect man who set unreasonable standards, who commanded his hangers-on to be as perfect as his father was, and yet met their inevitable failures with unmeasured forgiveness. Now, he is my reason for forward motion; then, all I had was a two-dimensional cardboard cut-out, meek, mild and totally voiceless.

The period in my life when I was at university was probably the furthest that I have ever been from God, I expect many have found the same. I made it through most of it without giving God a second thought. But towards the end of my time I would find myself awake in the middle of the night, or caught off guard with my thoughts straying onto something bigger than the sum of what my life added up to. Eventually after finishing my degree and leaving the country I met God 6,000 miles from home, in the last place I expected to find him. It turns out he likes to chase.

Working with some very poor young people, I found myself challenged about the system of values I had discreetly created and I decided that I wanted to know what a life worth living looked and felt like. On Sunday mornings I found myself rolling up to the church where some of my colleagues went. Often I would go to services in the local slums and it seemed at every moment someone around me was talking about God. In a short space of time I found myself part of a small group of people who I could relate to, despite our different backgrounds, nationalities and levels of faith, and whether we were leaning over a beer or an open Bible. Reading that book I found a man worth following and with him a hundred questions about whether I really could. I found a community of people willing to listen, looking outwards and wanting to know God better today than they did yesterday. I saw church how it was intended to be.

*Today, I co-lead an 'experimental' church plant in a city-centre pub in my spare time. Essentially it's a church for people who don't like what they have seen of 'church' and we get a variety of types. Some have had no previous Christian contact in their life; others have and were either mistreated or didn't 'fit in'. As you can imagine they bring their questions and frustrations, they are totally unin-terested in church culture, unfazed by our attempts to be 'relevant', but they **are** interested in Jesus, and the question of whether he is. But there's another group, a group of people retesting the Christian faith, those that have heard it all before and went away only to find that nothing else out there makes sense. They've been there, they have the T-shirt and they want something more. Most will have a moment in their life when they realise they're in a pigpen and they fancy* *going home. I have a lot of time for prodigals. I've seen what God can do when they come back.*

If I've learnt anything it's that God is totally concerned with us. We are unique. Your four-teen-year-old son or daughter who won't talk to you over the tea table is unique (you may not find that hard to believe) and is the total preoccupation of God. Sometimes it's helpful to remind ourselves of that. Too often we can read the story of the prodigal son and forget that it is allegorical. The temptation is to think of it only as an example of how we should forgive our children, forgetting that it's actually an example of how God forgives his. This stands as a lesson about how God waits, and the kind of party he throws when we come home.

I believe that God has great things in store for prodigals. He wants to mould them, but not crush their personalities. He wants them to bring their talents, experiences and their new-found passion, as well as their questions and frustrations, and put them to work in the family business – the kingdom of heaven, here and now, then and forever.

CHAPTER FOUR

It's Time to Stop Judging and Start Sharing

One of the clearest recollections of my young life is of a church meeting on a September evening. For the previous few years there had been an undercurrent of dissatisfaction with the leadership and now it was all coming to a head. This was high noon and the flock were going to tell the shepherds exactly what they thought. And some of them did – including a man who told one of the leaders that as his teenage son was going through a rebellious patch that leader was not fit to lead the church. I can remember watching as the leader answered as graciously as he possibly could, but his embarrassment was evident for all to see.

His embarrassment was evident for all to see

A silence descended on the meeting. It was as if somehow we knew that something was happening which was either wrong or foolish. In truth it was both. The man who spoke had made two mistakes: first with his interpretation of the Bible, and second that his own children were toddlers at the time. If you are to criticise anybody else's children you should always wait until your own are in their nineties – anything less exposes you to the possibility of a diet of your own words. Kids change. And so whether they are at present breaking our hearts or seem like visiting angels, it's best to remember that in the words of one of America's greatest baseball players, Yogi Berra, 'It ain't over till it's over.'

'It ain't over till it's over'

That kind of judgment comes easily because there are times in the Christian community when we give the impression that if we follow a certain set of guidelines it will guarantee that our children will turn out to be everything we ever hoped for. A friend of mine was recently asked to give a sermon entitled 'How to Bring up Godly Children.'

Are there really steps we can take, programmes we

can follow or biblical injunctions that we can adopt that will help us build a strong foundation for our children's lives? Yes, there are.

Is it possible to teach our children lessons about God, others and themselves that will stand them in good stead through the whole of their lives? Of course.

Can we co-operate with the Holy Spirit in doing our part as parents to help our children love God and want to serve him? Absolutely.

But we cannot, and we are fools if we think we can, do certain acts, parent in a certain way, even pray certain prayers, that allow us to say categorically: '*This* is how to bring up godly children.'

There are parents who have got it more right than most but whose children have turned their back on everything they hold dear, and there are those who have got it more wrong than most whose children serve God faithfully today. You and I cannot bring up godly children; it is not our responsibility – it is too heavy. We are called instead to live godly lives.

I remember a Christian leader's wife saying to me some years ago, 'Considering your involvement with Care for the Family, wouldn't it be ironic if your kids went off the rails?'

I may have imagined it, but as she spoke I thought I saw a glint of hope in her eyes that they *would*. I replied, 'It wouldn't be ironic at all. My wife Dianne and I have given the task of parenting our very best shot but there are no guarantees.'

Dianne and I thank God for every evidence we see in our kids' lives that God is at work, but I could not have written this book if there had never been a time when we had cried over them. What I said all those years ago in reply to that woman is still true – there are no guarantees – and our children, as do all of us, follow Christ a day at a time, with many a fall, and every step by the mercy of God.

The time has come to let the masks drop

Many of us need to repent of the way we have judged other people's children and instead begin to support each other. The time has come to let the masks drop, to begin to say, 'me too', and to set each other free from the intolerable burden of being the perfect parents. The wonderful thing is that when we are honest with each other, when we pray for each others' children, then their successes are not a threat to us but a joy – for they bring us hope for our own kids.

Some time ago I received this letter. The father who wrote it told me to use it to bring encouragement to others:

> *Last November our two eldest children, Brian and James, were convicted of crimes and both received prison sentences. My wife and I have tried to bring up our children on Christian principles so it came as a very big shock when our sons followed this lifestyle.*

> *Brian is in a young offenders' prison and James is in an adult prison which means that they have been separated since conviction.*

We have a very supportive church family

> *Although our sons' lifestyles for a while have been very different from ours we have remained a close family. We have a daughter, Carol, aged fifteen,*

and we have all visited as much as we can. Brian and James seldom ask for others to use their visit allowance.

We have not met any parents in our situation so we have not been able to learn directly from the experience of others, but we have a very supportive church family. One thing that we believe has been key, and led by God, has been our honesty and openness in talking about this. We kept the church informed and told our employers and colleagues about our sons' trouble. I felt it was important that I did not keep it a secret from my workmates; they were my friends and they knew my family and cared about us.

Our strength has come from our honesty

So many people told us that they admired our bravery but what we feel is that our strength has come from our honesty rather than us having the strength to be brave. God encouraged us to be open and he has carried us through this situation in a way that we have been able to encourage others. We have had people confide in us of situations they have kept hidden and carried as burdens for years and we are so grateful that God has spared us from that.

I know that we can't wear our hearts on our sleeves with everybody, and the truth is that some people simply won't be able to handle what we may be going through with our children, but there will be other hurting parents in your church, and certainly in your neighbourhood, with whom you can share. Meet with them, pray with them, laugh and cry with them. The Bible says we should 'bear one another's burdens'. That means to actually lighten the load. But there is an important qualification we must have if we are to do it. It was Thornton Wilder who said, 'In love's service, only the wounded soldiers can serve.'

It has always been so in the kingdom of God.

Prayer

*Lord, forgive the way we've judged
  each other.
We've all done it.
At times when our family life was going
  well,
Commented, carped, and sometimes enjoyed
  too much the giving of advice.
Well, Lord, now all that is gone.
We have no illusions about our right to
  preach, or teach, or criticise.
We have cried, are wounded now ourselves.
Lord, don't let this pain be wasted.
Let it rather cause us to go to those we
  might have criticised
And throw our arms around them,
  hold them near.
As we sustain each other and cry out
  together from broken hearts,
'Lord, have mercy.'*

Reflection

Praise be to the God and Father of our Lord Jesus Christ, the Father of compassion and the God of all comfort, who comforts us in all our troubles, so that we can comfort those in any trouble with the comfort we ourselves have received from God.

2 Corinthians 1:3–4

'In love's service, only the wounded soldiers can serve.'

Those who have been wounded and live with the scars often have the greatest understanding of the pain of others. It is more than having an experience in common, or showing empathy. It can be a 'fellowship of suffering'. We feel bound to one another by invisible, but invincible cords.

The knowledge that another understands our pain can be liberating. The pain may not go away, but suddenly it becomes bearable.

Thank God for someone with whom you share, or have shared, a fellowship of suffering, or pray that he will bring someone alongside you with whom you can discover it.

CHAPTER FIVE

Release the Life-Changing Power of Forgiveness

If love is the greatest power on the face of the earth, then forgiveness is the second greatest. Without forgiveness we die inside. With it, the memories may still be there but we can at least begin to move on. But for those who cry for prodigals there are sometimes so many things to forgive.

Without forgiveness we die inside

Sometimes we have to forgive those who have hurt those we love. My deepest gratitude and lifelong debt is to those who have been there for my children, and my deepest wounds have been at the hands of those who have hurt them. We may blame others for being part of our prodigals' rebellion, for being judgmental when they should have been supportive, for the comments they made to us at our lowest moments when we so desperately needed their comfort – but we must forgive them – even if that person is our husband or wife – we must stop nursing the hurt. We have to let it go.

And although we love them, we sometimes still have to forgive our prodigals for they may have treated us badly. They may have thrown our love, care and most fervent desire for their good straight back in our faces. And we must forgive even when they are still hurting us. We may want to say, 'If only he would stop that lifestyle, or give up the drink or the drugs', or 'If she would only get rid of the man who seems to be draining her of life, then we would forgive', but we must forgive even when there is no evidence that they may change.

We must forgive even when there is no evidence that they may change

What is the alternative to forgiveness? It is rejection. And rejection often brings with it isolation, bitterness, and a pushing even further away of those we are trying to draw back. One young man wrote to his parents that he was going to marry his fiancée with or without their approval. He may have been both headstrong and insensitive but even so the letter he got back from his father took his breath away. It read: 'Don't worry about inviting us to the wedding. We no longer have a son.'

Forgiveness allows us to go on loving. There is no greater exhibition of love than the death of Jesus, but that love could only flow because even as they were still banging nails into his hands and feet he cried out, 'Father, forgive them.' Forgiveness is not Disney World – it finds itself in the real world of deep hurts, dashed hopes and broken promises. But there is no hope for our prodigals without it.

> *Forgiveness allows us to go on loving*

Ernest Hemingway wrote a short story set in Spain in which a father and son fell out to such an extent that the son ran away to Madrid. The father said he wanted nothing more to do with him. Years later, the father realised he had been too harsh and wanted to put things right. He put an advert in a Madrid newspaper: 'Paco, meet me at the Hotel Montana at noon on Tuesday. All is forgiven. Papa.'

But Paco is a common name in Spain and when the

father turned up at the hotel he had to force his way through a crowd: all young men, all called Paco – and all longing to be reconciled with their fathers.

Of course, there may be another who needs forgiveness, for in spite of all I have said about being free of guilt there are moments when we may feel we have wronged our children – that our behaviour has been part of their being in some 'distant country'. Perhaps it was our legalism, our controlling nature, or the affair we had, that conspired to drive them away. Whatever we have done we must ask for God's forgiveness, and then the forgiveness of our prodigals. It may be hard to ask the forgiveness of someone who is hurting you so much but it is such a powerful thing to do. And sometimes it robs our prodigals of the very reason for their rebellion.

Whatever we have done we must ask for God's forgiveness

And then finally God's grace will allow us to do the hardest thing of all – to forgive ourselves. And when that happens the parable suddenly comes alive in a new way, for as we look at the figure coming down the road, we suddenly see that the dirty, tear-stained face is *our* face; it is *we* who are coming home full of shame and hearing the Father say, 'Put a robe on his back, shoes on his feet, and a ring on his finger.' And it is then that we discover what, deep in our heart, we knew all along:

We are the prodigal.

Prayer

Gracious God,
Give us the grace to forgive our child.
To let go of the hurt, the broken promises,
  the unfulfilled dreams.
For without forgiveness love will die,
  when it **must** live.
The future will be filled with bitterness,
  when it must be filled with hope.
As they mock, pour scorn, and steal our
  very dignity, help us forgive.
For if they don't know our forgiveness,
  they will not know our love.
And our love may be all they have.
Father, help us forgive them – for they
  know not what they do.

Reflection

If we claim to be without sin, we deceive ourselves and the truth is not in us. If we confess our sins, he is faithful and just and will forgive us our sins and purify us from all unrighteousness.

1 John 1:8–9

How great is the love the Father has lavished on us, that we should be called children of God.

1 John 3:1–2

'We are so busy being parents that we forget that all along what God wants most from us is for us to be his children.'

'… And it is then we discover what, deep in our heart, we knew all along: We are the prodigal.'

You can always come home

As you pray for the prodigals who are on your heart you may like to reflect on the following letter, written by a mother who is a friend of mine. You may even make it your own and send it.

You might be surprised to hear from me. It is some time since we spoke, even longer since we were together. But I have rewound and reworded our last conversation and relived our last meeting many times in my heart and imagination.

Words passed between us which would have been best left unsaid. Others could have built bridges across which to reach each other but were dismissed before they ever reached our lips. I painfully regret both.

But not all the memories are painful. I often wind the tape back

further like video film and watch
you as a child, clambering on a
rocky beach, or running with an
excited smile to show me some
treasure. I can still feel your hand
in mine as you urged me to hurry
along a windy street or held me
back because you wanted to watch a
tiny insect on an even slower
journey. I remember you as you grew.
The challenges you faced and the
friends you made. The pride I felt.

Then I wonder when things started to
go wrong. When we stopped talking
and started shouting. When even the
shouting gave way to silence, and the
silence to absence.

You have walked a path in these last
days that I would not have chosen
for you. But, as you often said, it is
your life and you must choose for
yourself, and I have accepted those
choices, however different they might
be from my own.

I want you to know that my love for you is greater than those differences. That despite all that has built a barrier between us, the love I have for you is strong enough to move it, even if piece by piece, and however long it takes.

Both of us need the forgiveness of the other. We still need to hear the words we've longed for. I believe it's never too late.

You may choose to ignore these words. They may make you angry, rekindling memories that you thought you had long forgotten. I understand that. But as your mother I can do nothing but go on loving you, go on asking for your forgiveness, and offering mine to you. No matter what has happened in the past and whatever is going on in your life right now, I love you, I am here for you and you can always come home.

Mum

CHAPTER SIX

Get the Home Ready for Their Return

I will never forget a prophecy given by an old man: 'When the Father's house is filled with the Father's love, the prodigals will come home.' If he is right then perhaps the greatest obstacle to the return of our prodigals is the state of the church.

When I meet people who have decided to stop attending church they rarely tell me it is because of some crisis of faith or disappointment with God. No, it is *We have somehow made it hard for them to stay* much more likely that they will talk about relationships within that church and sometimes of the person who hurt them deeply. This is never easy to deal with because it is possible they expected too much of others and, of course, are rarely without blame themselves. Nevertheless we have somehow made it hard for them to stay and sometimes almost impossible for them to return.

One of the most sobering aspects of local church life is the realisation that the way we have dealt with each other has caused some of our children to turn their back on what we believe. Through much of their young lives they have seen Christians fight each other and argue over the insignificant. They have silently watched as church members, including, perhaps, their parents, have criticised each other, hurt each other, and ostracised those they were meant to love. We forget that such attitudes make it very hard for others to follow Christ. One of Jesus' final prayers was: 'Father, I pray that they may be one, that the world may believe that you sent me.'

'Father, I pray that they may be one'

There is something mystical about the way that Christians relate to each other that authenticates the very love of God to people, and yet it is in the area of love at local church level that there is often such difficulty. Wherever I travel I find churches splitting. There are arguments over styles of worship, youth programmes or building schemes. Many leave their local church and join another, only to leave the new church after a few years because that one, too, has failed to meet their demands.

Many of us have developed a critical spirit in our dealings with others that makes it hard for our children to believe that God can love unconditionally. I urge parents not to criticise church leaders or other members of church in front of their young children. There is many a Sunday lunch table that is filled with conversation about what is wrong with the preaching, the music, or how hopeless the youth leader is.

You and I do not have the right to belong to a church that suits us in every respect. The great tragedy of much of church life today is that we have come to believe that 'church is for us'. We may have evangelistic programmes and a myriad of other activities but in our hearts we have a view of what suits us and woe betide the leadership if we don't get it. But it was never meant to be like this among us. This is how Paul describes the quality of relationship that demonstrates to a broken world the very love of God:

> *Love from the centre of who you are ... Be good friends who love deeply; practise playing second fiddle ... Bless your enemies; no cursing under your breath. Laugh with your happy friends when they're happy; share tears when they're down. Get along with each other; don't be stuck up. Make friends with nobodies; don't be the great somebody. Don't hit back; discover beauty in everyone. If you've got it in you, get along with everybody. Don't insist on getting even; that's not for you to do. 'I'll do the judging,' says God. 'I'll take care of it.'*

Romans 12:9–12 *(The Message)*

'Don't insist on getting even; that's not for you to do'

I think now of a teenage girl whose experience of church wasn't like that at all. In fact she saw her father, the church leader, driven to a nervous breakdown because of the pressure of dealing with the most bitter and sustained criticism. When Lucy, at age sixteen, vowed never to darken the door of a church again, it wasn't God she was turning her back on, it was the local church.

The scary thing about bringing up children is that they so easily catch our values. They watch the way we deal with each other and draw from that a view of how God deals with us. If you want children to grow up to believe that God could never love them if they get it wrong, then let them hear you pull apart the daughter of one of the PCC who has just got pregnant. There is many a prodigal who has gone even further away because, on the basis of what they saw in their young years in church, they believed that once you fell, there was no way back. The opposite is also true. When they see us try to stand for truth with compassion and utter love, they come to believe this is how God will act towards them.

It wasn't God she was turning her back on, it was the local church

My mind goes to a situation where a church leader was discovered to have had a severe lapse of moral judgment. The newspapers were full of the story and Christians too seemed to be having a field day talking about where he had gone wrong. The ten-year-old daughter of another church leader came home from church one Sunday and said to her father, 'Dad, people in church are saying that man has done really bad things.' Her father thought for a moment and then replied, 'Darling, he *has* done bad things, but if he honestly asks for God's forgiveness then God will gladly welcome him home.'

That leader said to me later, 'When my daughter spoke to me about it that day it was practically a holy moment. Of course I disapprove of what this man has done, but if I just joined in with the condemnation what would that have said to my daughter if ever she falls? I want her to know there is always a way back.'

Stop judging so much and above all forgive each other

If you would be truly radical, then do what Jesus said and invite your enemies to your parties. Be more tolerant of differences among each other, stop gossiping, and 'Don't bad-mouth each other, friends. It's God's Word, his Message, his Royal Rule, that takes a beating in that kind of talk. You're supposed to be honoring the Message, not writing graffiti all over it' (James 4:11, *The Message*). Stop judging so much and above all forgive each other. When you do such outrageous things you may still not end up with the church of your dreams – but your prodigals will come home.

Prayer

Lord, we repent of the state of your house.
Your dying prayer was that above all it
should be filled with love.
We have filled it with programmes,
meetings, minutes, and agendas,
But the love is hard to see sometimes.
What things we do to one another.
How easily we gossip, slander, stamp
and kick to get our way,
And wound those you have died for.
Sometimes it is easier to survive the world
outside than your church within.
Forgive us. And especially forgive us if
our criticism, our biting tongues, our
lack of love,
Has made it easier for some soul to leave
your house or harder to return.
And help us to change. To lay aside the
judging, and the petty fights and
squabbles
And lay a table, make a feast, pin some
ribbons on the door.
And yell into the darkness of the night,
'Give us another chance – to love you
and each other.
The house is not perfect, but it is swept
and cleaned, and a lamp is lit.
Come home.'

Reflection

> *Father, the time has come ... My prayer is not for them alone. I pray also for those who will believe in me through their message, that all of them may be one, Father, just as you are in me and I am in you. May they also be in us so that the world may believe that you have sent me.*
>
> John 17:1, 20–1

Within twenty-four hours of this prayer, Jesus was both dead and buried.

'When the Father's house is filled with the Father's love the prodigals will come home.'

What can I do in my local church to increase this love and hasten their return?

Julie's Story

When I was fourteen my parents, who were hard-working and, I suppose, what you might call 'dynamic' church leaders, moved our family abroad to take up a new job in church leadership. I found it really hard leaving my old school and friends. I felt very vulnerable and very insecure. There were lots of problems. The other kids in my school were stinking rich, while we weren't. Everyone hung out together after school, smoking cigarettes. I felt totally out of it. I needed acceptance and couldn't compete. Being a Christian felt so difficult and so irrelevant and that's when things started to go wrong, the beginning of me getting lost. I remember being in a café with about five other girls and asking for a cigarette. They wouldn't let me have one unless I learnt how to inhale. The irony was that they didn't want me to waste their cigarettes.

I stayed at that school for two years and then went to another one. That was hell. I remember

I used to cake myself in white make-up both to hide and to blend in with the others.

When I went to college to do A levels I met a girl – Karen. She was cool. I don't know what it was. I remember having a conversation with her at school and anyway for some reason I thought that she wouldn't be a virgin. So I told her that of course I'd lost my virginity at fifteen and that's when the lying started. I began to develop a secret life away from my parents. I was sinking. Not able to compete and be perfect, feeling rubbish academically and a general let-down. It drove me into hiding in a different world.

Karen and I had 'fun' – kissing boys, clubbing. I remember one time Dad coming up to my bedroom, sitting on the edge of my bed and telling me he didn't want me to go clubbing. I was saying, 'No, of course not', but secretly thinking, 'Oops, hope he doesn't find out I went last night.' Looking back it was awful. Karen had the use of her father's credit cards and, well, I just used to lie to my parents in order to be able to go out and enjoy our outrageous lifestyle.

Karen got me into modelling as well. She had all this expensive photography gear so she took seventy-two shots of me sprawled over park benches – provocative head shots, pouty, sexy shots. I remember taking them back and showing Mum and Dad who then promptly confiscated them, saying that they were pornographic. Looking back, they probably were. They weren't beautiful; I looked ill and unhappy; too thin.

I was doing really badly at college. The only friends I had seemed to be Karen and boyfriends. They didn't care about me though. I didn't know how to communicate with my parents; my denials and deceit had put up a huge barrier between us, so I kept running away.

I started skiving school. I spent days in a row trawling round the city just so I didn't have to go to school and sit at lunch on my own and face the consequences of not having done my homework. I sat in cafés, with hardly any money. The days were so long. I missed displaying my A-level art work because I thought it was just rubbish, and nearly failed. My spiritual life was non-existent. My relationship with my parents was all lies and I saw no way out – there were so many times when I just ran away from home or didn't come home. And yet my parents were trying so hard to show me their love for me and I would often come home to notes from Mum. Unfortunately I was past knowing how to communicate. I felt so dirty and so sad. So it went on.

One day I ran away and the person who I'd gone to stay with felt so guilty about Mum and Dad not knowing where I was that she rang them up. I remember Dad turning up and talking to her husband through the door, pleading to see me, and me refusing. Eventually though I agreed to talk to him and we went to a café. I remember Dad just telling me how nothing mattered but that I went home.

Anyway that night Dad was so loving, so kind, reaching out to me, meeting me halfway, wanting me home.

But my lifestyle continued the same. I remember so many things: after one guy practically forced me to have sex, drinking because I knew I'd been soiled and feeling like I couldn't go home, so fleeing to the local park, looking a wreck and feeling a mess. I remember getting picked up by some guys in a nightclub, going to a dark alley to smoke dope and get high and having sex with them – then having to have an AIDS test (and the torment of waiting for the result).

Anyway I was feeling dead inside. I hated all the lying and I hated myself. A hunger was beginning to grow inside me, a hunger for something real, something to live for, something to die for. And so it was that I was out one very wet evening, puffing on the end of a damp cigarette when I found myself heading for the Stream (a Saturday night youth service). I hadn't been for months and so this was so bizarre. I can remember going in and sitting at the back, my hair hanging down around my face and concealing it.

It happened during the worship. It was as though the heavens opened. There was a bright beam of light and heat that was coming down from on high. It was as if there was no one else there except me and God. And he was saying,

'You are mine.' It was like real fire falling down from heaven and my tears began to fall as I said sorry to God for not loving him and praying that I could know him. And I can remember just saying yes to God that evening and saying yes to coming home. It's like God was saying, 'It's alright, I'm going to meet all your needs and longings.' And as the tears fell and the repentance started I felt so forgiven, so loved by God. He just kept saying, 'You are mine' and I was replying, 'I am yours.' It was so freeing. It was so wonderful.

And afterwards I told my parents I was sorry, told them everything and watched them as they, too, cried. And I learned that when they had prayed, things had happened – like the time when I'd run away. They'd prayed that they would find me and my friend had rung them to tell them where I was.

God is so amazing. Those days of insecurity, of lack of confidence, of lack of hope and lack of freedom, seem so far away. I have just walked into his plan and he has opened up door after door. I have been able to do a foundation course and am *now doing a degree course. I met Peter and now we are married. We ran a group for fifteen- to eighteen-year-olds in our home and it was great to meet the kids and be real with them. I was really able to identify with them and it's just wonderful seeing them come to know the Lord and being able to pray with and talk to them about life.*

My parents were fantastic through it all. They never stopped praying – and I know they never would have stopped, ever – not until I'd come home.

CHAPTER SEVEN

The Patience to Wait and the Grace to Accept

All my adult life I have been captivated by the picture of the father in the parable running down the road towards his boy. When the old man reaches him he throws himself on his son and begins kissing him. It is a wonderful image. A friend illuminated it even more for me. He said, 'It is a remarkable kiss – because of the pigsty.'

I said, 'What do you mean?'

My friend said, 'The boy would have smelt of the pigsty, but the father didn't even mention it. He put a robe on top of those filthy clothes, a ring on the hand that was still stained with the swill, and shoes on the feet that had shared the mud with the animals. He could

'It is a remarkable kiss – because of the pigsty'

have said to the servants, "Quick! Run a bath for my son!" and to the boy, "As soon as you're cleaned up come into the house." But this old man was wiser than that. He knew that he must be patient; that even when the physical smell of his son's wanderings were gone, that it would take time to leave it all behind. The prayers weren't all answered yet. The journey didn't end with the boy coming down the road. This was going to take time.'

When our prodigals come home we need to be patient with them

When our prodigals come home we need to be patient with them. Let not the first thing we say be, 'I hope you've left that life behind forever.' They may be bruised and scarred, hurting and confused. We can't expect them to have it all sorted out immediately. Some of them are not even sure of what needs to be sorted out. They don't necessarily want to put on a Sunday suit, rush to the prayer meeting, or say grace at the meal table, but they do know that more than anywhere else on the face of the earth they want to be home.

I think of one prodigal who said, 'Be patient with

me, Dad. I know there's lots wrong with me, but I do want to get my life turned around and get right with God again.' In many ways it is rather like that other parable; they need a Samaritan who is willing to pour oil in their wounds, to love them, and give them rest.

Many of the prodigals I have met over the years have been people who have been Christians for years but have been bruised or broken in some way – perhaps by other Christians. Others are desperately ashamed of what they have done. Sometimes they find the prospect of an immediate return to a local church just too daunting.

All who came were looking for a safe haven for a while

For many years Dianne and I held a weekly meeting in our home; we called it 'The Strugglers Group'. All kinds of people came to it: some were prodigals, often people in mid-life who had somehow lost their way in the faith and wanted to take a step back towards God but were not quite sure how to; others came who had spent all their lives giving to those around them and were now burnt out; some had no faith at all. But whoever they were and whatever their story, all who came were looking for a safe haven for a while.

The atmosphere was very accepting. We often studied the Bible but we were just as likely to simply talk together. We prayed together every week but not with any expectation that everybody would join in, and nobody was ever asked to prepare 'next week's topic'. The truth is we often didn't have a 'next week's topic'! We had few fixed agendas and frankly nobody was ever sure whether that night we'd end up discussing, 'Why does God allow suffering?' or watching a film on television. And we tended not to get too excited if somebody said something outrageous. After one woman had been coming for six months she said, 'On the first night I tried to shock you. But nobody took any notice.'

I suppose the key element is that we tried to love people just as they are, and whatever they were going through at that time. And we tried to be honest and *real* with each other. Over the years all kinds of people have asked to join the group and I have often wondered why some came who had vowed never to go into a church again. Some said it felt like home, but I think it was more than that. I have a hunch that when people let their masks down, including the leaders, and genuinely reach out to God and to each other, then so often Jesus himself meets with them. Many who came not only rediscovered their own faith but went on to help others in their journey. Some are now leading groups of their own.

'Mum, I can't explain this but I really believe that God is speaking to me'

Many prodigals have a clear view of where they have gone wrong and people have not been reticent in pointing out where that was, but even as they tried to make their way home, they have sometimes found it hard to find encouragement. You may have a daughter who has been a prodigal. She has lived a selfish life, caring little for others. But one day she rings you up and says, 'Mum, I can't explain this but I really believe that God is speaking to me. I know I'm not like all the others that go to your church but I feel I must spend some of my time working with disadvantaged kids in the evenings. There's still a lot I'm not sure about but I've started praying in my room and asking God to forgive me, guide and help me. I know there's a long way to go, and I don't really understand all that's going on, but I feel the need of God.'

What that child needs is not a mother who says, 'That's wonderful. Will you be in church next Sunday?' But rather, 'Darling, this is what we have prayed for down the years. God has touched your life. We are so proud of what you are doing with those deprived kids. Let us know how we can go on praying for you.'

Be patient with them. And be patient, too, in your waiting – and yet look out for that action you can take which may hasten the return of your prodigals. It could be a letter, a visit, an apology, or perhaps just a phone call.

'This home is yours, the door is always open to you'

I remember speaking to a large group of church leaders; I was talking about how our kids can sometimes break our hearts. As I finished I said, 'Some of you may want to ring a son or daughter tonight and say, "I know you have turned your back on everything we have ever believed, but this home is yours, the door is always open to you. Forgive us if we have ever given you the impression it was otherwise. We love you."'

A few days later I got a letter from one of those church leaders. He said, 'We made the call that very night. We are beginning to rebuild a relationship we thought was gone forever.'

And sometimes acceptance means we have to learn to love those that they love. Peter and Hilary were faced one day with the news that their son, Daniel, was moving in with his girlfriend. Afterwards they stayed up most of the night and talked about it. They felt sadder than they had felt for a long time but in the early hours of the morning Hilary took her husband's hand and said, 'Peter, all my life I have prayed that Dan would marry somebody who followed Christ, but that might not happen. Dan loves her and I have decided that I *will* love her. And, if you can, I want you to join me in loving her too.'

'A relationship we thought was gone forever'

From that day on, every time Sally came to that house she was hugged and welcomed. Her birthday was never missed, her opinion was both sought and respected. In short, Peter and Hilary loved her – at first as an act of the will. And then one day Sally's parents suddenly broke up and a strange thing happened. She came straight around to speak with Hilary – she needed another woman. Hilary can remember holding her as she sobbed, and when Sally had gone, she turned to Peter and said, 'I love that girl, really love her, and I believe she knows it.'

One day after church somebody said to Hilary, 'I saw you out shopping with Sally the other day. How can you condone what she and Dan are doing?' Hilary thought for a moment and then said, 'I wasn't condoning it, I was shopping with her. And in every shop and over every cup of coffee I was saying, "I love you." And at first it was very hard – harder than you'll ever realise. But, you know, I am trying to be Jesus to that girl. And love is getting easier.'

And sometimes our prodigals need time. God is not in a hurry. Listen to his Word:

> *But these things I plan won't happen right away. Slowly, steadily, surely, the time approaches when the vision will be fulfilled. If it seems slow, do not despair, for these things will*

*surely come to pass. Just be patient! They will
not be overdue a single day!*

Habakkuk 2:3 *(Living Bible)*

And finally, remember the real reason why Jesus
told this parable: the entrance of the elder brother is
the dreadful sting in the tale and the awful
condemnation of those who are so concerned with
their own piety that they miss the breathless grace
of God to the prodigals: those for whom the rules
are more important than the forgiveness. He had
overheard the religious leaders complaining that he
was mixing with sinners and eating with them.
These teachers of the law and Pharisees are like
the elder brother with his whining,
complaining and careful guessing
of the sins that his younger
brother had committed: 'He has
squandered your money with
prostitutes.'

*Pray
with all your
hearts that they
meet the father
first*

That spirit is still with us and if your
prodigals do come home, pray with all your hearts
that they meet the father first and not the elder
brother. The elder brother will say, 'Nice to see you
back at church. But can I still smell alcohol on your

breath? And I hope you've broken up with that woman who was no good for you. Perhaps now you'll start taking your responsibilities here a little more seriously.'

Oh, that elder brother! The one who did his sinning without ever leaving. The one who needed to 'come home' every bit as much as his brother but who could never grasp what the heart of real love is – both to give and to receive it. The brother who never did get to a party – not even his own.

The sheer wonder of his son's return had swept away the pain

The elder brother simply couldn't understand the unconquerable nature of the father's love. No catalogue of rules broken, or pleas that it was all so unfair, can rob this father of joy. He is dancing with happiness: 'Son, but we had to celebrate. Your brother was dead and is alive again, he was lost and is found.' In a single moment, the sheer wonder of his son's return had swept away the pain of all the years of waiting, the gossip, the sleepless nights and the all-consuming fears.

It was over.

His boy was home.

Prayer

Oh Lord, I remember so clearly the first moment I held him. He was so tiny. I felt so proud and grateful to you for his safe birth. I prayed to you as I looked into his face, 'Lord bless this child and keep him safe from all evil. Be with him every moment of his life and may he grow to love and serve you.'

He's grown to be a good and loving son. I still feel so proud and grateful to you for him. He hasn't been to church much for a long time. Does that mean you're no longer with him – that he's never really loved you? – that he'll never serve you?

Lord, protect me from doubt and lack of faith. I will repeat the prayer I said on the day he was born every day of my life.

Reflection

For God is able to '… carry out His purpose and do superabundantly, far over and above all that we dare ask or think – infinitely beyond our highest prayers, desires, thoughts, hopes or dreams'.

Ephesians 3:20 *(Amplified Bible)*

Confirm, O Lord, that word of thine
That heavenly word of certainty,
Thou gavest it; I made it mine,
Believed to see.

And yet I see not; he for whom
That good word came in thy great love,
Is wandering still, and there is room
For fear to move.

O God of Hope, what though afar
From all desire that wanderer seems
Thy promise fails not; never are
Thy comforts dreams.

Amy Carmichael

Carol's Prayer

*I was thinking today, Lord, of when my sister
and I were little girls and how we used to share
a bed. That bed was where our mother sat with
us to read Bible stories and where we said our
prayers. It was the bed where some nights we
kicked each other and sometimes we cried in
some shared childish upset, or laughed together
till Dad came to the bottom of the stairs and told
us to go to sleep. It was where we talked about
you, Lord. Where we wondered and questioned
and grew to love you.*

*And then came the day when the bed was taken
from our room and two brand new ones replaced
it. We felt so grown up and excited. That night
we had to talk a bit louder to each other to make
ourselves heard across the room.*

*But as the years went by I realised there was a
more important separation between us and I
remember the first shock of awareness that it
wasn't **our** faith anymore, it was **my** faith.*

Suddenly we were different from each other as never before. The core of my being, the thing most precious to me – my knowledge that you loved me – was something she didn't share, something she said she'd 'outgrown'.

We are so close. So much has happened – terrible times and wonderful times – and mostly we've been through them together. But it's not enough, Lord.

I want her back, Lord. I want it so much. I want her to know what it's like to be loved by you and to be forgiven. I want her to be safe, healed, made whole. I want her to love you.

It hurts. I feel so angry and frustrated and guilty... and it's scary that she still seems such a long way from you. It's hard to keep praying with faith, Lord.

Be with her, Lord. She's my sister. Bring her home soon.

CHAPTER EIGHT

Praying Home the Prodigals

The date was 14 March 1998. Dianne and I had been asked to speak at an event called 'Bringing Home the Prodigals' at the National Exhibition Centre in Birmingham. When we arrived we knew that this was to be a Saturday of prayer with thousands of people gathered from all over the United Kingdom to ask that God in his mercy would reach out to the prodigals and bring them back. What we *didn't* know was that we were about to experience something that would touch our lives forever.

We were about to experience something that would touch our lives forever

After some worship and a period of individual and corporate prayer, the chairman invited people to take part in a very special act of petition. A huge cross, fifteen feet high, had been erected in a corner of the auditorium near the stage. On a table next to the cross were pens and small squares of paper. People were invited to come forward, write the names of the prodigals who were on their hearts, and place those names at the foot of the cross. They were then asked to stand near the cross and pray for them.

People flocked forward. After ten minutes or so one of the leaders turned to the speaking team on the platform and asked if we, too, would make our way to the foot of the cross and pray with those who were standing there. I have prayed with people during events like this many times in my life and I can't say that I felt anything very

People were bringing to God those who had broken their hearts

unusual as I made my way across the stage and down the steps leading to the floor of the auditorium.

But what I saw when I got near the cross stopped me in my tracks. There were already *hundreds* of names around the cross. People were bringing to God those who had broken their hearts – husbands, wives, friends, other relatives – but most of all the children. I suddenly started to cry, the tears causing the names to blur in front of my eyes. I tried to imagine the stories behind those names; what heartbreak lay behind the simple card that read, 'Pray for Tom to come home.' I simply could not stop crying. It was as if the pain of the world lay at the foot of that cross. And all around me people were praying – praying the same prayer, over and over again: 'Lord, bring back the prodigals.'

It seemed to me to be a truly supernatural event, filled with incredible power, and as I have considered why that should have been, a possible explanation has come to me. As those who have cried for prodigals, and especially the parents of prodigals, come to pray they often have a wonderful advantage: *they are humble*.

It seemed to me to be a truly supernatural event

These men and women have hearts that have been broken; they have learned that no person – no matter how gifted, no book or seminar, is going to bring the answer to their prayers; they are totally dependent on God.

I believe that God wants us and *likes* us to feel our need of him and when we are thrown completely on his grace – because there is nowhere else to go – he hears our prayers. I cannot promise you that your prayers will be answered in the way that you want, but I do know that when we feel that God is our only hope we are at the best place we can be.

> *If my people ... will humble themselves and pray ... then will I hear from heaven.*
>
> 2 Chronicles 7:14

It is significant that on that memorable day people laid the names of their prodigals at the foot of the cross. The cross of Christ is the greatest mystery in the world. It is a place of apparent defeat and yet unassailable victory; it is a place of tears and yet has in it the seeds of unbridled joy. The cross of Christ reminds us that the darkness of Good Friday gives way to the joy of Easter Sunday.

And there is no better place to bring your prodigal than to the foot of the cross. As we come with humble hearts to pray, we acknowledge that we have no answers, painful memories, perhaps little faith, and yet we commit those we love to Christ and ask that by his grace he will bring them home.

We are all on a journey, whether we are prodigals or those who pray for their return, and you and I have been on a journey together in this book. This path has led us to the cross. May I suggest that sometime soon you find a quiet place and bring the names of your prodigals to the foot of that cross.

We must somehow learn to leave those we love in the hands of God

Those who did so on that day in Birmingham wrote the names on paper, and left them there. That was very significant for two reasons: first, we must somehow learn to leave those we love in the hands of God; second, as we all left we were urged to take two or three names home with us and pray for them. And so we each began to bear one another's burdens and to lift to God the prodigals of others.

You may wish to do the same: to actually write down the names of those you pray for and having brought them to God, then give them to somebody else who will promise to pray. It may be that in churches all across the land, small groups will meet to pray for these precious ones.

> *Do not be afraid, for I am with you; I will bring your children from the east and gather you from the west. I will say to the north, 'Give them up!' and to the south, 'Do not hold them back.' Bring my sons from afar and my daughters from the ends of the earth.*

Isaiah 43:5

Remember that God loves your prodigals even more than you do

It is true that the parable we have considered together concerns a parent and child, but your prodigal may be a brother or sister, a husband, wife, friend or, even in a strange reversal of the parable – a mother or father. But whoever they are, and wherever they are, remember that God loves your prodigals even more than you do.

Never stop praying, don't ever give up.

And always leave a light on.

'The cross of Christ is the greatest mystery in the world. It is a place of apparent defeat and yet unassailable victory ...

... And there is no better place to bring your prodigal than to the foot of the cross.'

A Prayer for the Prodigals

Lord, only you know where our prodigals are – not just the physical place but in their hearts, their minds, their spirits. None of us can hide from you, and who is lost that you cannot find?

We pray for them. Lord, bring them home – not just to us, not even first to us, but to you. Forgive us if as parents, friends, or churches we have made it easier for them to leave or harder to come back.

Wherever they are and whatever they are doing, touch their lives. And when they come home give us the spirit of the father and not the elder brother.

And, Lord, there are some of us who to the outside world seem never to have left the father's house, but we ourselves know how far we have wandered. Bring us back also.

And when they come back, those who have gone far away and those who have wandered near, then teach us all that sometimes in your kingdom it's not another meeting we need – but a party.

BRINGING HOME THE
PRODIGALS

Bringing Home the Prodigals Project

This book is part of a major initiative by Care for the Family.

The project includes a website (www.prodigals.org.uk), events organised throughout the country and a national call to prayer for our prodigals.

Visit the website to:

- **Get up-to-date news on the project**
- **Send us your prodigal's story**
- **Find out details of *Bringing Home the Prodigals* events near you**

This book ends with an encouragement to bring our prodigals to the cross – the website gives us another opportunity to do just that.

For further details of the latest developments you can also write to Care for the Family, PO Box 488, Cardiff, CF15 7YY or telephone (029) 2081 0800.

Premier Christian Radio have a *Lifeline* for prodigals on 0845 3450707.